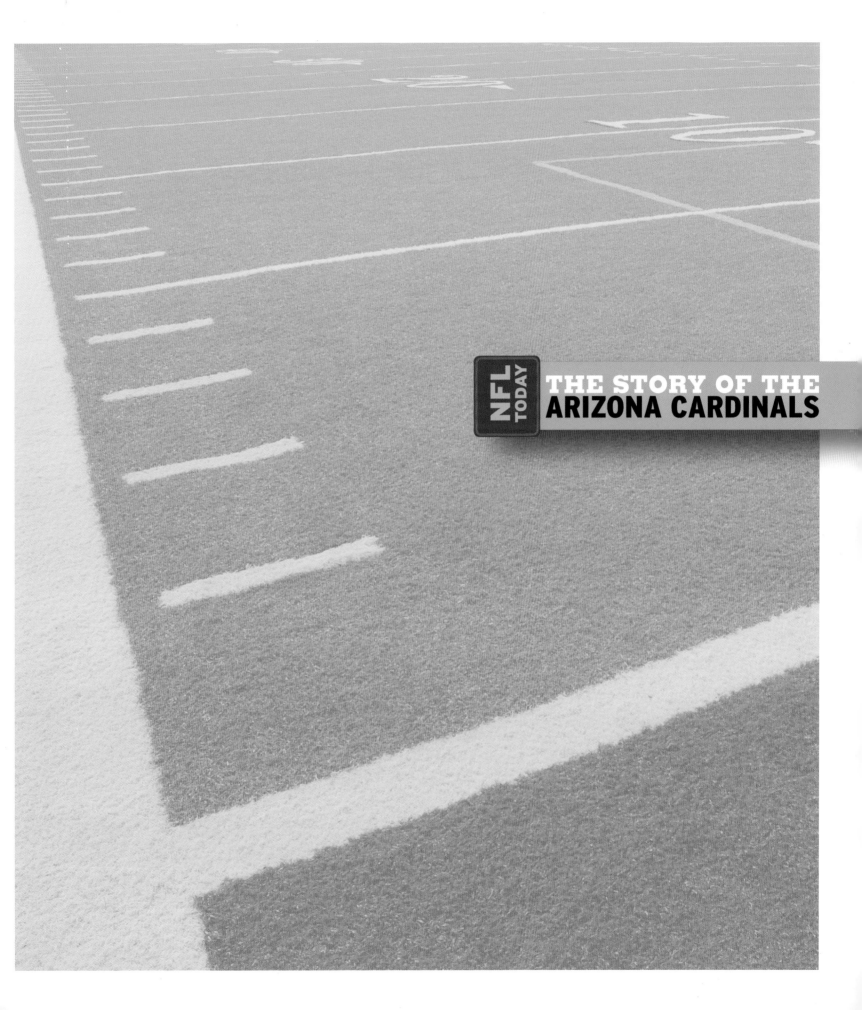

NFL TODAY

THE STORY OF THE
ARIZONA CARDINALS

NFL TODAY

THE STORY OF THE
ARIZONA CARDINALS

SARA GILBERT

CREATIVE EDUCATION

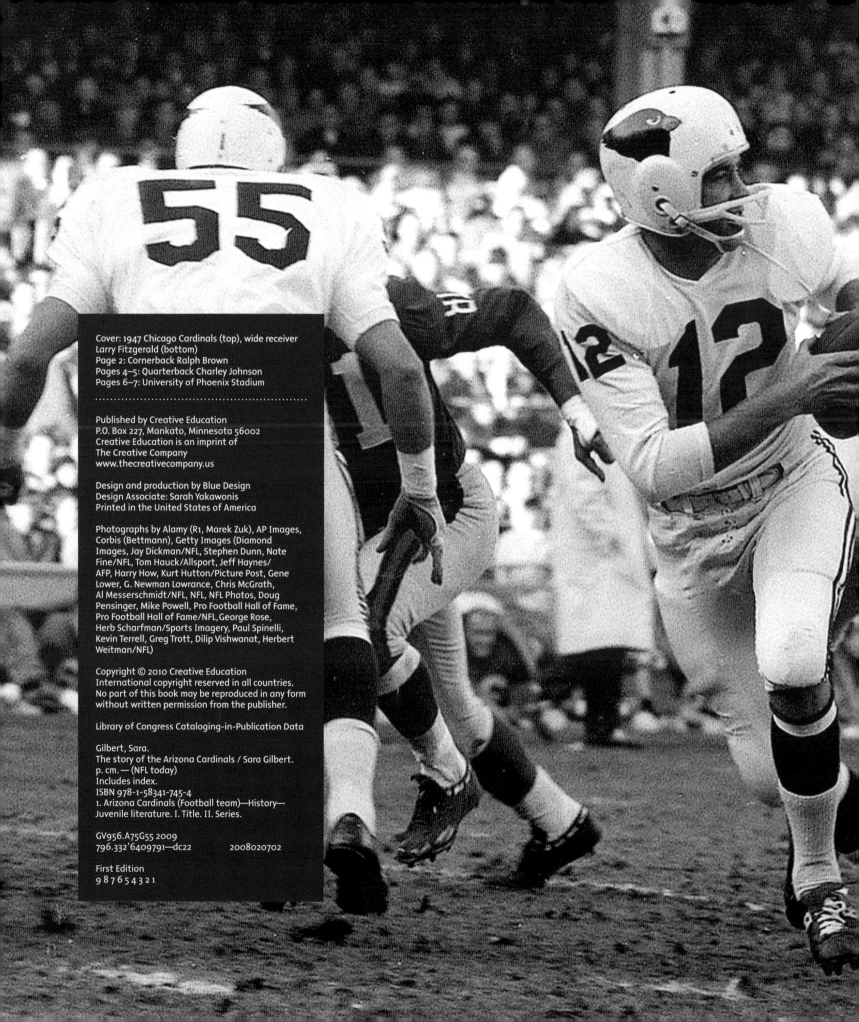

Cover: 1947 Chicago Cardinals (top), wide receiver
Larry Fitzgerald (bottom)
Page 2: Cornerback Ralph Brown
Pages 4–5: Quarterback Charley Johnson
Pages 6–7: University of Phoenix Stadium

....

Published by Creative Education
P.O. Box 227, Mankato, Minnesota 56002
Creative Education is an imprint of
The Creative Company
www.thecreativecompany.us

Design and production by Blue Design
Design Associate: Sarah Yakawonis
Printed in the United States of America

Photographs by Alamy (R1, Marek Zuk), AP Images,
Corbis (Bettmann), Getty Images (Diamond
Images, Jay Dickman/NFL, Stephen Dunn, Nate
Fine/NFL, Tom Hauck/Allsport, Jeff Haynes/
AFP, Harry How, Kurt Hutton/Picture Post, Gene
Lower, G. Newman Lowrance, Chris McGrath,
Al Messerschmidt/NFL, NFL, NFL Photos, Doug
Pensinger, Mike Powell, Pro Football Hall of Fame,
Pro Football Hall of Fame/NFL, George Rose,
Herb Scharfman/Sports Imagery, Paul Spinelli,
Kevin Terrell, Greg Trott, Dilip Vishwanat, Herbert
Weitman/NFL)

Library of Congress Cataloging-in-Publication Data

Gilbert, Sara.
The story of the Arizona Cardinals / Sara Gilbert.
p. cm. — (NFL today)
Includes index.
ISBN 978-1-58341-745-4
1. Arizona Cardinals (Football team)—History—
Juvenile literature. I. Title. II. Series.

GV956.A75G55 2009
796.332'6409791—dc22   2008020702

First Edition
9 8 7 6 5 4 3 2 1

CONTENTS

ON THE SIDELINES

MEET THE CARDINALS

WINDY CITY
RIVALRIES

In 1867, a Civil War veteran named Jack Swilling came upon a lush river valley in the midst of the Arizona desert. It looked like fertile farmland, because pumpkins were growing along a series of canals that had been built by American Indians who had since abandoned the area. Swilling wanted to call the new town Pumpkinville, but another suggestion won more support from his fellow settlers: Phoenix, for the mythical bird that is reborn from its own ashes. The name seemed fitting, as the settlement would be built on old Indian ruins.

The desert city has since risen out of those ruins to become a thriving metropolitan area. Today, Phoenix is known for its well-kept golf courses, year-round warmth, and beautiful desert landscapes. It is also known as a hot spot for sports fans, including followers of the Arizona Cardinals, a National Football League (NFL) franchise that moved to Phoenix in 1988. But the Cardinals are not a homegrown franchise. They started out far to the northeast, in Chicago, Illinois.

In 1898, a house painter named Chris O'Brien organized a group of men on the south side of "The Windy City" to play football. They called themselves the Morgan Athletic Club until they moved to Normal Field on Racine Avenue about a year later. But their new name, the Racine Normals, stuck only

X Set in a blazing valley, Phoenix experienced a rise in population—as well as in its appeal as a destination for sports franchises—in the mid-1900s with the development of air conditioning.

until they tried on a set of cast-off, maroon uniforms from the University of Chicago in 1901. "That's not maroon," O'Brien said. "It's Cardinal red!"

The Racine Cardinals, led by star halfback and quarterback John "Paddy" Driscoll and young running back Ralph Horween, joined the American Professional Football Association (APFA), a forerunner of the NFL, when it started in 1920. So did a crosstown club called the Tigers. O'Brien immediately challenged the Tigers to a high-stakes game; the winner could stay in the league, while the loser had to withdraw. Driscoll scored the only touchdown in the Cardinals' 6–0 victory.

But no sooner had the Tigers departed than a new rival came to town: the Chicago Bears. By 1922, the APFA had become the NFL, and the Bears and "Cards" were competing with one another on the field and at the ticket office. Between 1922 and 1925, the newly named Chicago Cardinals won three games and lost three games against the Bears, plus one tie. In 1925, the Cardinals' 11–2–1 record was the best in the league, earning the team the NFL championship.

Still, the Bears were winning the battle for fans. As attendance dwindled at the Cardinals' Comiskey Park, O'Brien ran short of money. In 1929, he sold the team to a Chicago doctor named David Jones, whose first move to rejuvenate

PADDY DRISCOLL

RUNNING BACK, QUARTERBACK
CARDINALS SEASONS: 1920-25
HEIGHT: 5-FOOT-11
WEIGHT: 160 POUNDS

It might not seem like much by today's standards, but the $300 John "Paddy" Driscoll was paid for each game he played for the Cardinals in the 1920s was a huge sum then. But Driscoll was worth it. He was an exceptional quarterback who could also run the ball and even play defense. His real skill, however, was in his kicking leg. Driscoll drop-kicked field goals with remarkable accuracy and sent punts amazing distances. In one game in 1925, he booted four field goals through the goalposts. On more than one occasion, he was responsible for all of the Cardinals' points scored in a game; in one game in 1923, he singlehandedly scored 27 points. Driscoll was especially effective against the Cardinals' crosstown rivals, the Bears. In 1922, he scored all the points accumulated in both matchups between the two teams—six in one game and nine in the other. That made it all the more painful to fans when, in 1926, the Cardinals traded him to the Bears. Driscoll played four more seasons in Chicago before retiring in 1929.

[11]

A CONTROVERSIAL CHAMPIONSHIP

In the NFL's early days, league champions were crowned on the basis of their final record—not the results of playoffs and a championship game, like today's Super Bowl. The team with the most wins in a season was awarded the title. And in 1925, that team was the Chicago Cardinals, which boasted an 11–2–1 mark. The title was disputed by the Pottsville (Pennsylvania) Maroons, who had a 10–2 record and had beaten the Cardinals decisively in the final game of the season. But NFL president Joseph Carr had suspended the Maroons because they had played an unauthorized exhibition game. When Chicago was declared the champion, Cardinals owner Chris O'Brien refused to take the disputed title. The Cardinals accepted the title when the Bidwill family took ownership of the team, but Pottsville fans still protest the decision. In 2003, the NFL reconsidered the ruling but voted against reversing the decision. "[Pottsville] was a championship-caliber team that ran into an unfortunate conflict with the league's rules," NFL commissioner Paul Tagliabue said. "At this late date, it was impossible to overturn."

the club was to coax 26-year-old fullback Ernie Nevers, who had previously starred for the Duluth Eskimos, out of an early retirement.

Nevers turned the much-anticipated matchup between the Cardinals and the Bears on Thanksgiving Day, 1929, into a one-man show. Behind Hall of Fame guard Walt Kiesling's power blocking, Nevers scored every Cardinals point in a 40–6 victory. He rushed for six touchdowns, kicked four extra points, and set an NFL single-game scoring record that still stands. All that legendary Bears coach George Halas could say about the game was, "The final score: Bears 6, Nevers 40."

X Called "the football player without a fault" by legendary college coach Pop Warner, the great Ernie Nevers excelled at every facet of the game, including punting.

The Cardinals finished 6–6–1 in 1929. Then, even with the fine play of versatile kicker and receiver Roy "Bullet" Baker, the team went a middling 10–10–2 over the course of the 1930 and 1931 seasons. In 1932, Nevers retired once again.

Nevers's departure coincided with the arrival of a new team owner: Charles W. Bidwill Sr., who paid Jones $50,000 for the Cardinals. By 1935, Bidwill's Cardinals had improved to 6–4–2. Unfortunately, the team couldn't keep the momentum going long enough to win another championship in the 1930s. Even bringing Nevers back as a coach in 1939 didn't help. The team managed only one win that year.

World War II hit the Cardinals hard in the early 1940s, as many of Chicago's top players left football behind to serve in the military. In 1943 and 1944, the Cardinals posted a combined 0–20 record. Then, on October 14, 1945, with more than 20,000 Bears fans at Wrigley Field expecting to see a blowout, rookie quarterback Paul Christman led the Cardinals to a 16–7 victory over their crosstown rivals. Although that was the team's only win in 1945, it snapped a 29-game losing streak and established Christman as the Cardinals' quarterback of the future.

CHARLES W. BIDWILL SR.

TEAM OWNER
CARDINALS SEASONS: 1932–47

Charles Bidwill (pictured, right) loved football. He had been a vice president of the Chicago Bears before an opportunity came up that he couldn't refuse: owning a professional football franchise, even if it was his team's crosstown rivals. Bidwill left the Bears and their winning record to buy the struggling Cardinals for $50,000 in 1932. Although that losing trend continued for most of his tenure as owner, Bidwill never lost hope or gave up on his team. But like any good businessman, Bidwill wanted to see a return on his investment. So, in 1946, he entered a bidding war against the New York Yankees football team (a franchise in a competing pro league) to sign Charley Trippi (pictured, left), a high-stepping, fast-as-lightning halfback from the University of Georgia. After the Yankees maxed out their offer at $75,000, Bidwill presented a $100,000, 4-year deal to Trippi, believing that Trippi would lead the Cardinals to a championship. He was right, but he didn't live long enough to see it. In April 1947, Bidwill died at the age of 51. His team won the NFL championship just eight months later.

CHAMPIONS AGAIN

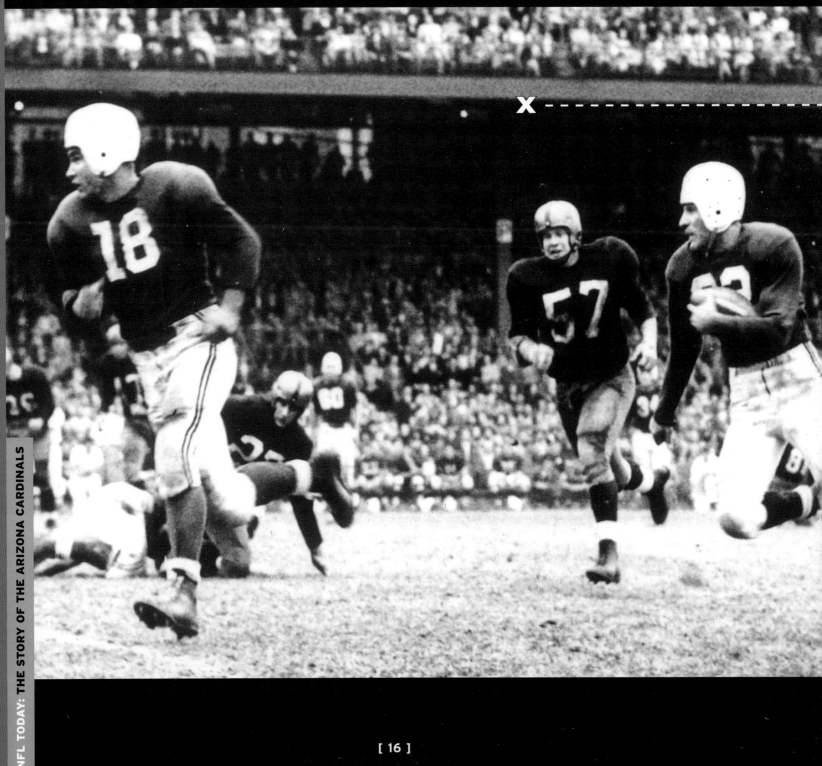

Cardinals coach Jimmy Conzelman had plans for Christman in the late 1940s. Although the young quarterback was notorious for fumbling the football, Conzelman saw potential in his passing skills. The coach converted the team's offense to a T-formation around the strong-armed quarterback. In this formation, churning fullback Pat Harder lined up directly behind Christman, with halfbacks Elmer Angsman and Marshall Goldberg on either side of him. In 1946, that combination led the Cardinals to an improved 6–5 record, including a glorious 35–28 victory over the Bears in the final game of the season.

That promising finish inspired Bidwill to invest more money in the club's roster. Before the 1947 season, he signed Charley Trippi—a sensational running back from the University of Georgia who was being courted by teams in both the NFL and the rival All-America Football Conference—to a contract worth $100,000. The amount was a small fortune in those days, but Trippi was worth it to the Cardinals.

The "Dream Backfield"—as the combination of Christman, Harder, Angsman, and Trippi was known—led the Cardinals to a 9–3 record in 1947. In the final game of the season, the Cards met the Bears in a battle for the Western Division title, with the winner to go on to the NFL Championship Game. The

Cardinals opened the game with an 80-yard touchdown pass from Christman to speedy halfback Boris Dimancheff, then intercepted four Bears passes. Their 30–21 victory earned them the division crown and a matchup with the Philadelphia Eagles for the league championship.

That game, played on a frozen field at Chicago's Comiskey Park, was bittersweet. The Cardinals won 28–21, thanks to scoring runs by Trippi and Angsman and a fourth-quarter interception by Goldberg, who also played defensive back. But Bidwill was not around to see it happen. He had died before the season started, leaving the team in the hands of his wife, Violet.

The Cardinals enjoyed another outstanding season in 1948, compiling an 11–1 record that still stands as the best in franchise history. Chicago again took on Philadelphia in

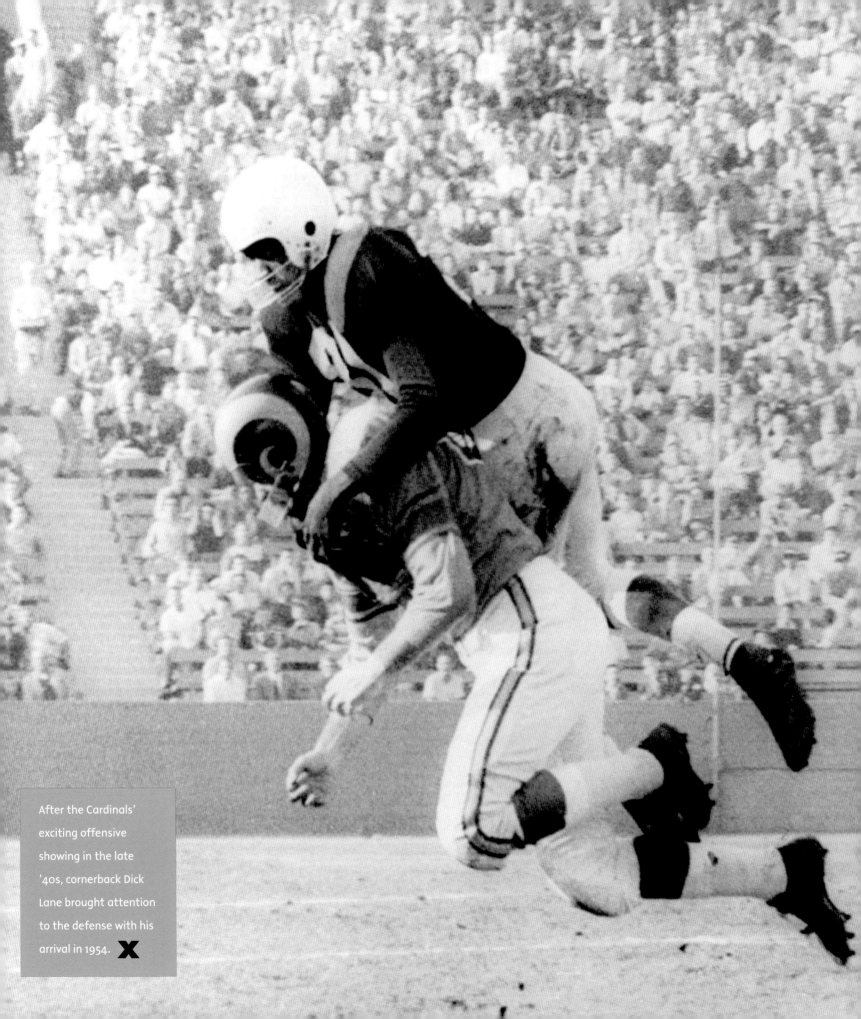

After the Cardinals' exciting offensive showing in the late '40s, cornerback Dick Lane brought attention to the defense with his arrival in 1954. **X**

WARTIME MEASURES

When the United States entered World War II in 1941, thousands of American men dutifully reported for service. Almost 1,000 of them were players, coaches, or managers from the NFL, including more than a dozen from the Chicago Cardinals. Offensive end Keith Birlem, defensive end Chuck Braidwood, halfback Chet Wetterlund, and coach Jack Chevigny were among the 20 men from the NFL who were killed in action. While they were fighting in Europe and the South Pacific, their teammates back in Chicago were trying to field a team. It became so difficult to keep enough men in the lineup that, in 1944, the Cardinals combined forces with the Pittsburgh Steelers and played as the Card-Pitts. The team was co-coached by Chicago's Phil Handler and Pittsburgh's Walt Kiesling, who had once played for the Cardinals. Only 7,000 fans showed up when the team, which split its home schedule between Comiskey Park in Chicago and Forbes Field in Pittsburgh, played in Chicago. The Card-Pitts didn't win any games that season, leading some frustrated fans to mockingly call the 0–12 club the "Carpets."

the title game. But as a blizzard blanketed Philadelphia, the Eagles scored the only touchdown of the game and won 7–0. Coach Conzelman retired after the season, exhausted by the challenges of keeping the Cardinals competitive. "It's a rough business, this winning," he said.

A 6–5–1 season in 1949 was the Cardinals' last winning effort for several years. Even with the likes of speedy running back Ollie Matson and punishing defensive back Dick "Night Train" Lane, the Cardinals would tally a miserable 33–84 record throughout the 1950s. As the last game of the 1953 season, against the Bears at Wrigley Field, approached, the Cardinals were still winless for the year. Head coach Joe Stydahar was determined to win—and he threatened to withhold his players' paychecks if they lost. The motivated Cardinals rallied to win that game, 24–17, ending the season 1–10–1.

By 1959, things had gotten ugly in Chicago. While the Bears enjoyed successful seasons and a packed stadium, the Cardinals were losing both games and fans. Matson was traded to the Los Angeles Rams as the team lost 10 of 12 games that year. Revenue plunged, making it clear that Chicago couldn't continue to support two teams. So the Bidwill family announced that the Cardinals would be moving to St. Louis, Missouri, where another Cardinals team was already playing baseball, in 1960.

STARTING OVER
IN ST. LOUIS

The change of scenery did the Cardinals good. In 1960, running back John David Crow emerged to set a team single-season rushing record with 1,071 yards, and wide receiver Sonny Randle led the league with 15 touchdowns. The team, which shared Sportsman's Park with the baseball-playing Cardinals, won just six games but gained thousands of new fans that first season in St. Louis.

Aside from a woeful 1962 season in which owner Violet Bidwill died and the Cardinals went 4–9–1, the team settled into a winning groove that would last for most of the decade. The defense was anchored by safety Larry Wilson, who frequently helped quarterback Charley Johnson and the rest of the offense by intercepting passes and returning them for touchdowns. Wilson's intensity impressed both teammates and opponents. Former New York Giants coach Allie Sherman once called him "the goingest player I ever saw."

Despite their improved play, the Cardinals' playoff drought continued. Then, in 1966, the Cardinals signed an unknown and undrafted quarterback named Jim Hart. Hart, who

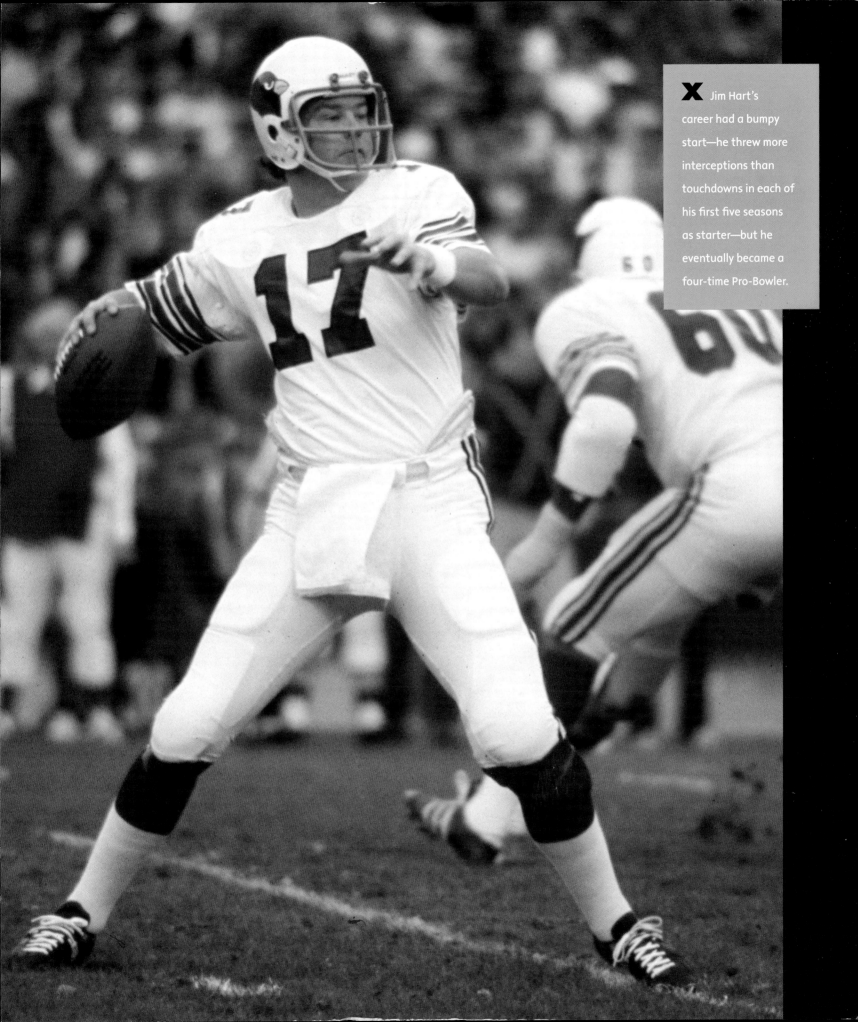

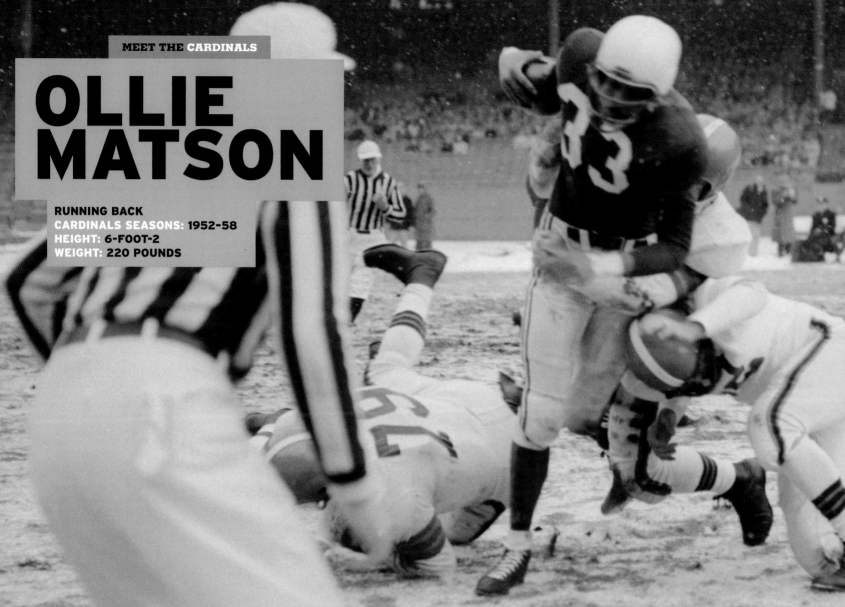

OLLIE MATSON

RUNNING BACK
CARDINALS SEASONS: 1952-58
HEIGHT: 6-FOOT-2
WEIGHT: 220 POUNDS

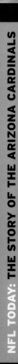

Ollie Matson was the Cardinals' first-round pick in the 1952 NFL Draft. But the fleet-footed star from the University of San Francisco couldn't sign his contract immediately. First, Matson wanted to run as a member of the U.S. track team in the 1952 Summer Olympics in Helsinki, Finland. He won a bronze medal in the 400-meter race and a silver medal in the 1,600-meter relay, then brought his world-class speed to Chicago. As a rookie, Matson earned both Pro Bowl and All-Pro honors. He trained on sandy beaches during the off-season to challenge himself and pick up more speed each year. In his six years with the Cardinals, he totaled 3,331 rushing yards and 40 touchdowns. "I'm disappointed if I don't make a long run in a game because I know people come and pay their good money to see me make long runs," Matson once said. "I like to please them." So large was Matson's role in the offense that when the Cardinals traded him to the Los Angeles Rams in 1958, they received nine players in return. In 1972, Matson was inducted into the Pro Football Hall of Fame.

would play 18 seasons in St. Louis and set most of the team's

passing records, was soon joined by speedy wide receiver

Mel Gray, halfback Terry Metcalf, and an offensive line led

by mountainous tackle Dan Dierdorf. Although the Cardinals

remained outside the playoffs for the rest of the decade, they

became an exciting team to watch. The club developed such

a knack for come-from-behind victories (and suffered more

than a few frustrating near misses along the way) in the late

1960s and early '70s that the media began calling them the

"Cardiac Cardinals."

All the heart-pumping action culminated in 1974,

when the Cardinals won their first seven games and finished

the season 10–4, good enough to win the National Football

Conference (NFC) East Division championship. For the first

time in 25 years, they were in the playoffs. The Minnesota

Vikings defeated the Cardinals in the first round of the 1974

playoffs, but St. Louis players and fans believed the franchise

had turned the corner.

When the Cardinals won the division again in 1975, fans

really began to believe, even though St. Louis lost 35–23 in the

playoffs to the Rams. The 1976 season started well, with the

Cards reaching midseason at 5–2. Then a controversial missed

pass interference call in a Thanksgiving Day game against

BOUGHT BY THE BIDWILLS

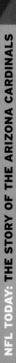

The same family has owned the Cardinals for more than 75 years. That stretch of continuous ownership began in 1932, when Charles W. Bidwill Sr., a vice president of the Chicago Bears, decided to buy his team's fiercest competitors, the Chicago Cardinals. Bidwill was willing to spend money to turn the team into a champion, which eventually happened in 1947. By then, however, Bidwill had passed away and left the team to his wife, Violet. All that time, their two boys, William ("Bill") and Charles Jr., had been sitting through practices and serving as ball boys during the games. So when Mrs. Bidwill, the first female owner in the NFL, died just two years after managing the team's move from Chicago to St. Louis in 1960, it was only natural that she would leave the team to her sons. In 1972, Bill and his family became sole owners of the team, while Charles became managing general partner. By 2008, another generation was involved as well: Bill's son Michael Bidwill (pictured) was then the president of the team.

the Dallas Cowboys led to a loss that eventually bumped the

10–4 team out of playoff contention. "It's a shame," general

manager Joe Sullivan said as the season ended. "This is the

best team we've had."

By the end of 1977, however, that team was falling apart.

St. Louis couldn't manage a winning record, much less a

playoff berth, until the strike-shortened 1982 season, when

the 5–4 Cardinals were among 16 teams invited to a special

Super Bowl tournament. In the first game, the Cardinals fell

41–16 to the Green Bay Packers.

In 1983, with young quarterback Neil Lomax connecting

with All-Pro wide receiver Roy Green for 1,227 yards and a

X Small but speedy, Terry Metcalf treated Cardinals fans to some electrifying performances as a rusher, receiver, and kick returner.

X Roy Green made a strong case as the best receiver in football in the mid-1980s; he led all NFL wideouts in touchdowns (14) in 1983 and receiving yards (1,555) in 1984.

league-leading 14 touchdowns, the Cardinals put together an improved 8–7–1 record. But neither that nor the team's 9–7 record in 1984 could get St. Louis back to the postseason. Injuries to Lomax, Green, and running back Ottis Anderson stalled the Cards in 1985, and the team couldn't recover.

Like the Chicago fans before them, St. Louis football fans seemed unwilling to suffer through any more losses. By 1987, team owner William "Bill" Bidwill, the son of the late Charles Bidwill, was frustrated by the city's refusal to replace Busch Stadium, which held fewer fans than all but one other stadium in the NFL. He started looking for sunnier skies under which to play.

X Before joining the Cardinals, quarterback Neil Lomax made headlines in college by once throwing seven touchdown passes in a single quarter.

PHOENIX RISING

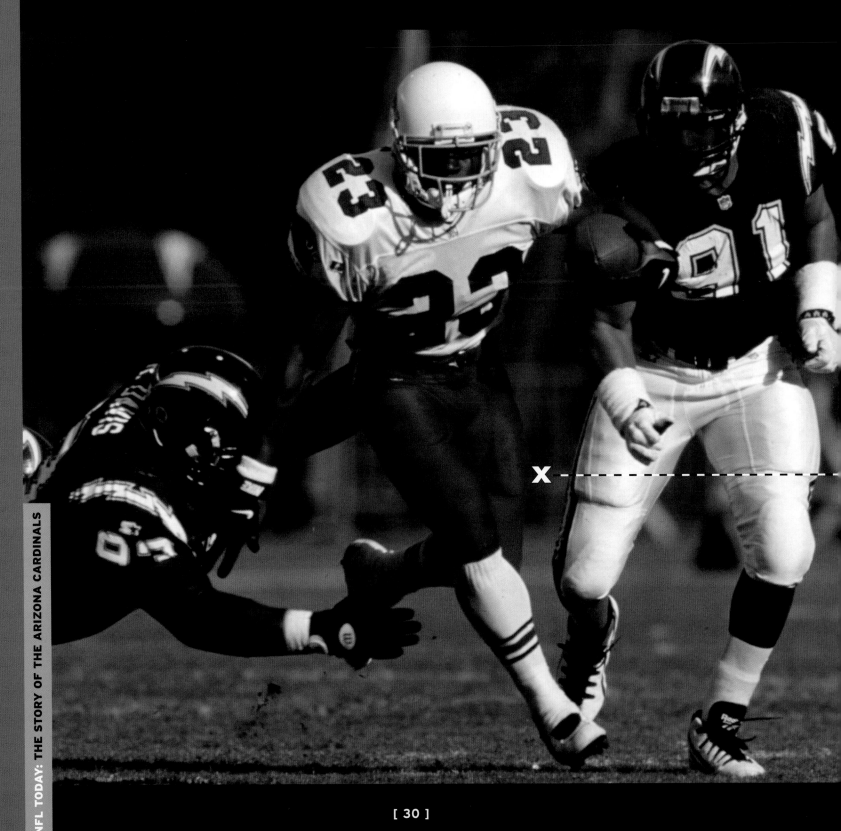

Bidwill found those sunny skies in Phoenix, Arizona. The Phoenix Cardinals' new home, in Sun Devil Stadium on the campus of Arizona State University (located in nearby Tempe), was full for the team's first home game, a 17–14 loss to the Dallas Cowboys on September 12, 1988.

Lomax, Green, and explosive wide receiver J. T. Smith gave their new fan base something to cheer about, as Lomax threw for nearly 3,400 yards in just 14 games. Although the 1988 season ended with five consecutive losses and a mere 7–9 record, the team set a single-season franchise record for attendance at 472,937. Arizona seemed like a happy home.

Lomax's happiness didn't last long, however; an arthritic hip forced the 30-year-old quarterback to retire before the start of the 1990 campaign. Then Green was traded after the team suffered through a miserable season. With veteran leadership in short supply, the Cardinals lost the last eight games of the 1991 season to finish 4–12, a record that was duplicated in 1992.

The team's rebuilding efforts, including the drafting of running back Garrison Hearst in 1993 and the hiring of defensive mastermind Buddy Ryan as head coach in 1994, helped the Cardinals climb out of the NFC East cellar. Now known as the Arizona Cardinals, the team improved to 8–8 in

X Halfback Garrison Hearst was selected with the third overall pick of the 1993 NFL Draft, but, hampered by injuries, he scored only four touchdowns in three seasons with the Cardinals.

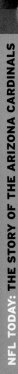

LARRY WILSON

SAFETY
CARDINALS SEASONS: 1960-72
HEIGHT: 6 FEET
WEIGHT: 190 POUNDS

Larry Wilson was known to his teammates as "Wildcat," and it was a nickname that fit him well. The tall, lanky safety was as tough as a tiger—and as intimidating to his opponents as well. Cardinals defensive coordinator Chuck Drulis named a play that called for the free safety—usually Wilson—to blitz the quarterback "Wildcat" in Wilson's honor. Wilson perfected the new, unexpected play throughout the years. But it was his ability to steal the ball out of the air that opposing teams feared the most. Wilson snagged 52 interceptions during his 13-year career, returning them for a combined 800 yards and 5 touchdowns. In one 1965 game, with both wrists broken and covered in casts, he intercepted a pass—a demonstration of toughness that coaches have used to motivate ailing players ever since. Wilson ended his playing days in 1972, but he returned to the Cardinals as an interim coach in 1979 and then joined the front office staff in 1980. After 43 total years with the Cardinals, Wilson, who was voted into the Pro Football Hall of Fame in 1978, retired in 2002.

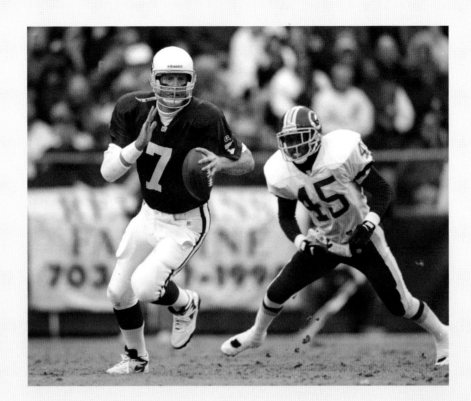

1994. But as Hearst recovered from a knee injury and Ryan's motivational tactics failed, Arizona fell back to the bottom of the standings in 1995.

The 1996 season started with a new coach, Vince Tobin, and a new quarterback, Boomer Esiason. Although Esiason, who had led the Cincinnati Bengals to the Super Bowl a decade earlier, was nearing the end of his career, he led Arizona on a three-game winning streak that included a 522-yard passing performance (third-best in NFL history) against the Washington Redskins. With the defensive talents of hulking tackle Eric Swann and crafty cornerback Aeneas Williams, the Cardinals rebounded to finish the season a respectable 7–9.

But as Esiason contemplated retirement in the off-season, Coach Tobin knew that the offense needed a spark. And in

X Boomer Esiason made his single season in Arizona a memorable one with his amazing passing performance against the Redskins.

X Jake Plummer used both his feet (217 rushing yards) and arm (547 passes) to help lead the Cardinals to the postseason in 1998.

the 1997 NFL Draft, the Cardinals thought they had acquired that spark in Arizona State University quarterback Jake Plummer. Known as Jake "The Snake" (a nickname his brothers gave him after catching him reading a book about another NFL quarterback, Ken "The Snake" Stabler), Plummer had led the Sun Devils to an undefeated season in 1996 and a berth in the Rose Bowl. By 1998, Plummer had also led the Cardinals to a 9–7 record and their first playoff appearance in 16 years.

The Cardinals came out strong against the Cowboys in the playoffs. Behind solid efforts from Plummer and running back Adrian Murrell, Arizona took a 20–0 lead and won 20–7, its first postseason victory in 51 years. Finally, after so many

TURKEYS FOR THE CARDINALS

Thanksgiving Day games have often been memorable for the Cardinals, beginning way back in 1929, when halfback Ernie Nevers singlehandedly scored 40 points to beat the Bears before sitting down to enjoy his turkey and stuffing. Later holidays, however, were not so kind to the team. On Thanksgiving Day 1976, the Cardinals took an 8–3 record to Dallas. With the game on the line, tight end J. V. Cain was heading for the end zone and what looked to be a game-winning touchdown catch when he was shoved out of bounds by two Cowboys defensive backs. Although it appeared to be pass interference, no penalty was called, and the Cardinals lost both the game and the chance to make the playoffs that year. In 1977, the Cardinals were in the midst of a six-game winning streak when the Miami Dolphins came to town for Thanksgiving. The day belonged to Dolphins quarterback Bob Griese, who threw six touchdowns in Miami's 55–14 rout of St. Louis. That loss demoralized the Cardinals, starting a 12-game losing streak that extended into the 1978 season.

JACKIE SMITH

TIGHT END
CARDINALS SEASONS: 1963-77
HEIGHT: 6-FOOT-4
WEIGHT: 235 POUNDS

Jackie Smith had good hands. The Cardinals relied on those hands to haul in receptions and on his fast feet (Smith was also a track standout in college) to reach the end zone once he made the catch. Smith, who played all but the final year of his NFL career with the Cardinals, finished his career with 480 receptions for a total of 7,918 yards (the most by a tight end in the NFL until 1990) and 43 touchdowns. But he was such a versatile athlete that he was also handed the Cardinals' punting duties during his first three seasons. Although he was a pivotal player in the Cardinals' two playoff appearances in the 1970s (1974 and 1975), it is his postseason play with Dallas that most fans remember. In 1978, Smith signed with the Super Bowl-bound Cowboys. He dropped a third-down pass late in the Super Bowl, forcing the Cowboys to kick a field goal. When Dallas lost by four points, Smith became the scapegoat. He retired from football before the next season started and was inducted into the Hall of Fame in 1994.

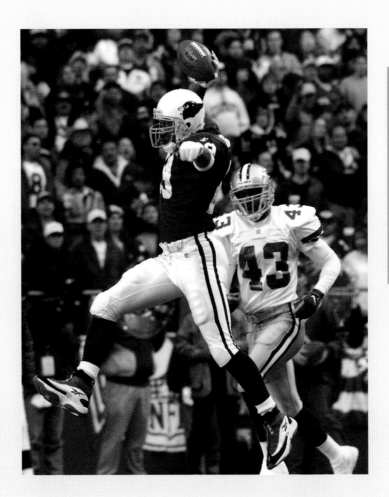

down years, the Cardinals had something to celebrate. "The past is the past," Plummer said. "You live in the present. Now, we are ready to go into the future." The future that season was short-lived, though, as the Cardinals lost to the Vikings a week later. But, for the time being at least, hope had been restored in Arizona.

Unfortunately, that sense of hope quickly evaporated as the Cardinals returned to their losing ways. In the middle of the 2000 season, Coach Tobin was dismissed, and the Cardinals tumbled to last place in the NFC East with a 3–13 mark. Plummer's star, too, had fallen. In 1999, the gunslinging quarterback threw 24 interceptions and only 9 touchdown passes. In 2002, after Arizona's third consecutive last-place finish, he left the team to play for the Denver Broncos.

The Cardinals replaced him with journeyman quarterback Jeff Blake, who helped mentor young draft pick Josh McCown. In 2003, the team also made headlines by signing former Cowboys running back Emmitt Smith, who was the league leader in all-time rushing yards and touchdowns. Although Smith was 34 years old, the Cardinals believed the future Hall-of-Famer still had some great performances in him. With promising young receiver Anquan Boldin also added to the lineup, Arizona expected a marked improvement. Boldin had an immediate impact in 2003, tallying the most receptions (101) by a rookie receiver in NFL history. But Smith was sidelined with a shoulder injury, and the Cardinals went just 4–12.

As construction began on a new Cardinals stadium in Glendale, just west of Phoenix, the team hired the 33rd coach in its history. That coach was Dennis Green, who had previously

X Anquan Boldin stunned the NFL with his record-setting rookie season; many scouts had thought the strapping wide receiver was too slow to become dominant at the pro level.

led the Vikings to the playoffs 8 times in 10 years. "I'm here for one reason," Green said as the season started. "Because I believe with all my heart that we can build ourselves an outstanding program."

But no matter how much Green believed, Arizona wasn't ready to be a champion. In 2004, the team mourned the loss of former safety Pat Tillman—who had quit football to join the U.S. Army and was subsequently killed in Afghanistan—but couldn't even win the game at which they honored the fallen hero. Despite the outstanding play of defensive end Bertrand Berry, who led the NFC with 14.5 sacks, the Cardinals finished 6–10, well out of playoff contention.

With McCown struggling, the Cardinals brought in veteran quarterback Kurt Warner, a two-time NFL Most Valuable Player (MVP), in 2005. But neither he nor All-Pro running back Edgerrin James, a free-agent signing in 2006, could get the Cardinals above the .500 mark. Even moving into the luxurious new University of Phoenix Stadium in 2006 wasn't enough. By the end of a 5–11 season in 2006, Coach Green had lost both his patience and his job. The Cardinals started the 2007 season under new head coach Ken Whisenhunt.

With Whisenhunt at the helm and quarterback Matt Leinart, a first-round pick in the 2006 NFL Draft, leading the

HOME SWEET HOME

There wasn't much excitement for the Arizona Cardinals or their fans in 2000, when the team lost all but three of its games. But the Cardinals scored a major victory that year when the citizens of Maricopa County, where the franchise is based, voted to help fund a new stadium for the team. The Cardinals, who had never played in a park of their own design, took the opportunity to dream big about what it would include—and most of their wishes came true. When the finished product was unveiled six years later, the University of Phoenix Stadium had both a retractable roof and a retractable natural grass field that could be moved in its 17-million-pound tray outside the stadium's walls to flourish in the sun when the team was not playing. Perhaps more importantly, the stadium had additional seating, which the owners hoped would translate into additional revenue and, in turn, a more competitive team. "There is a direct correlation between revenue from new stadiums and being able to compete," said team president Michael Bidwill. "The teams with new stadiums are consistently in the playoffs."

ON THE SIDELINES

A GAME OF SURPRISES

It was a surprising turn of events: The lowly Arizona Cardinals, owning a meager 1–4 record in early October 2006, were trouncing the undefeated and heavily favored Chicago Bears 20–0 at halftime of a game in Phoenix. Players, fans, and even the television announcers for Monday Night Football were shocked at the score. Unfortunately, things changed during the second half. Arizona fumbled twice, and both times, the Bears returned the ball for a touchdown. Then, with two minutes left on the game clock, speedy Bears punt returner Devin Hester danced into the end zone to give Chicago the lead, 24–23. Arizona drove the ball to the Bears' 41-yard line in the final minute, but kicker Neil Rackers missed a field goal try, sending the Cardinals to a heartbreaking loss. But what happened next was the biggest surprise. Angry and overcome with frustration, Cardinals coach Dennis Green pounded his fists on the podium during the postgame press conference. "The Bears are who we thought they were!" he yelled. "And we let 'em off the hook!" The tirade was widely televised, and after the Cardinals finished the season 5–11, Green was fired.

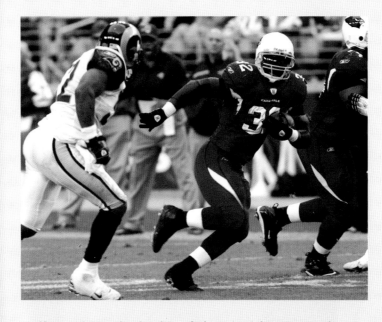

offense, the Cardinals rebounded to win eight games and finish in second place in the NFC West Division in 2007. Then, in 2008, Arizona really soared. Warner was named the team's starting quarterback and seemed to rediscover his old MVP form. As he slung the ball to a terrific trio of receivers in Boldin, Larry Fitzgerald, and Steve Breaston, the Cardinals won their division and returned to the playoffs. Few experts saw the Cardinals as a serious contender, but Arizona defied the odds, beating three playoff opponents—the Atlanta Falcons, Carolina Panthers, and Philadelphia Eagles—to reach the first Super Bowl in franchise history.

Super Bowl XLIII pitted the Cardinals against the Steelers, who featured the NFL's top-ranked defense. Arizona started slowly and trailed 20–7 in the third quarter. But behind Warner, who passed for 377 yards, and defensive tackle Darnell Dockett, the Cardinals staged a furious comeback, seizing a 23–20 lead on a 64-yard scoring strike to

X Although past his prime years, Edgerrin James was still going strong in 2006 and 2007, topping 1,000 rushing yards for the 6th and 7th seasons of his career.

X A Heisman Trophy winner and two-time national champion at the University of Southern California (USC), Matt Leinart was projected as Arizona's quarterback of the future.

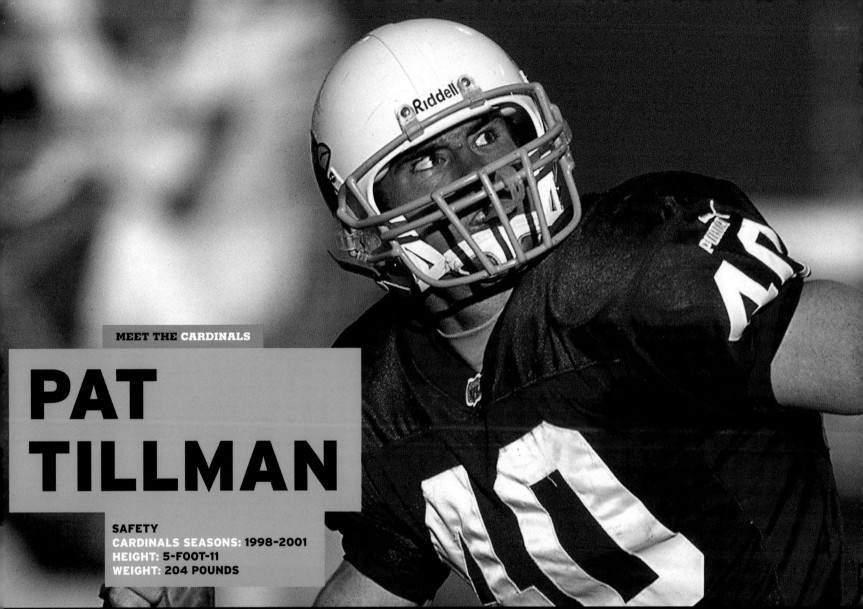

PAT TILLMAN

SAFETY
CARDINALS SEASONS: 1998–2001
HEIGHT: 5-FOOT-11
WEIGHT: 204 POUNDS

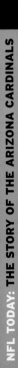

In the four short seasons that Pat Tillman played in the NFL, he accumulated 331 tackles, 2.5 sacks, 3 interceptions, and 3 forced fumbles. For a player who was drafted with the 226th overall pick in the 1998 NFL Draft, those statistics are impressive. But although many remember his scrappy playing style fondly, Tillman is better known for his decision to enlist, along with his brother Kevin, in the U.S. Army just eight months after the terrorist attacks against America on September 11, 2001. In 2003, he was sent to the Middle East as part of the invasion of Iraq known as Operation Enduring Freedom. He also served in Afghanistan, where, in an accident on April 22, 2004, he was shot and killed by a fellow soldier. On September 19, 2004, every team in the NFL honored Tillman by wearing a memorial sticker on their helmets, and the Cardinals retired jersey number 40 in his honor. "He represented all that was good in sports," Cardinals coach Dave McGinnis said. "He proudly walked away from a career in football to a greater calling."

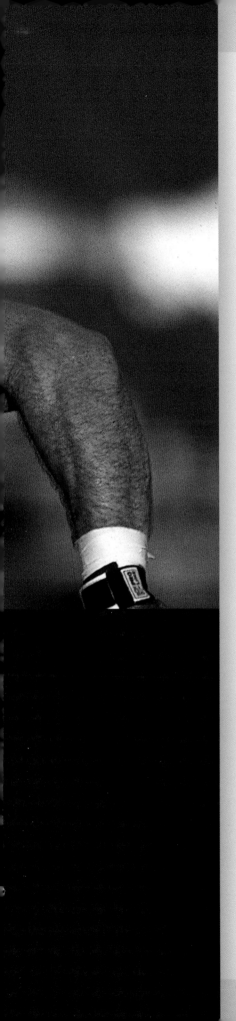

Fitzgerald late in the fourth quarter. But it was not to be. The Steelers marched down the field one last time to score the winning touchdown with just 35 seconds remaining. It was a heartbreaking loss for Arizona, but what a ride it had been. "I am so proud of this football team," Warner said. "We gave ourselves a chance to win a world championship, but that other team went out and won it."

For the Cardinals, the future is bound to be better than the past. The oldest continuously run professional football team in the U.S. is also the NFL's least successful franchise. The last time the team won the NFL championship was in 1947—more than six decades and two relocations ago. But like the mythical bird for which the team's current home is named, today's Cardinals have risen from the ashes and are hoping to soar back to the Super Bowl soon.

X The Cardinals started to fly high under coach Ken Whisenhunt, pulling away from the rest of the NFC West in 2008 to win their first division title in 33 years.

INDEX